LANDSCAPE
Gardening

WRITER
PHILIP HARDGRAVE

PHOTOGRAPHER
STEFAN HAMES

ILLUSTRATORS
PETE COLLINS
LUCY SARGEANT
LOIS LOVEJOY

AVON BOOKS ◆ NEW YORK

Acquisition, Development and Production Services by BMR, of Corte Madera, CA

Acquisition: JACK JENNINGS, BOB DOLEZAL

Series Concept: BOB DOLEZAL

Developmental Editing: BOB DOLEZAL

Photographic Director: ALAN COPELAND

Cover Photo: JIM GALLOP

Interior Art: PETE COLLINS

North American Map: RON HILDEBRAND

Copy Editing: NAOMI LUCKS, JANET REED

Proofreader: TOM HASSETT

Typography and Page Layout: BARBARA GELFAND

Index: SYLVIA COATES

Horticulturist and Site Scout: PEGGY HENRY

Color Separations: PREPRESS ASSEMBLY INCORPORATED

Printing and Binding: PENDELL PRINTING INC.

Production Management: THOMAS E. DORSANEO, JANE RYAN

Film: FUJI VELVIA

First Avon Books Trade Printing: February 1992

ISBN: 0-380-76665-5

Library of Congress Catalog Card Number: 91-67350

91   92   93   94   95   10   9   8   7   6   5   4   3   2   1

Special thanks to Strybing Arboretum & Botanical Gardens, Golden Gate Park, San Francisco, CA; University of California Botanical Garden, Berkeley, CA; The Davis Arboretum, University of California, Davis, CA; The Dry Garden, Berkeley, CA; Petri's Restaurant, Napa, CA; Mudd's Restaurant, San Ramon, CA; Mary Jobson, Sonoma, CA; Jerry Cichon, Sonoma, CA; Mr. & Mrs. Rankin, Santa Rosa, CA.

Additional photo credits: Kim Newton and Robert Frerck, Woodfin Camp & Associates, pages 8-9, for Spanish/Moorish and Formal Gardens. Bonnie Lee Appleton, page 36, for Fountaingrass. Robert Lyons, page 36, for Reedgrass. Michael Landis, pages 50-63, for Azalea, Dogwood, Ice Plant. Pam Peirce, page 51, for Camellia. Derek Fell, pages 54-59, for Lilac, Rhododendron, Sorbus, Redbud. Arizona-Sonora Desert Museum, pages 62-63, for Suguaro. Bob Dolezal, page 62-63, for Yucca.

AVON BOOKS
A division of
The Hearst Corporation
1350 Avenue of the Americas
New York, New York 10019

AVON TRADEMARK REG. U.S. PAT. OFF. AND IN OTHER COUNTRIES, MARCA REGISTRADA, HECHO EN U.S.A.

LANDSCAPE
GARDENING

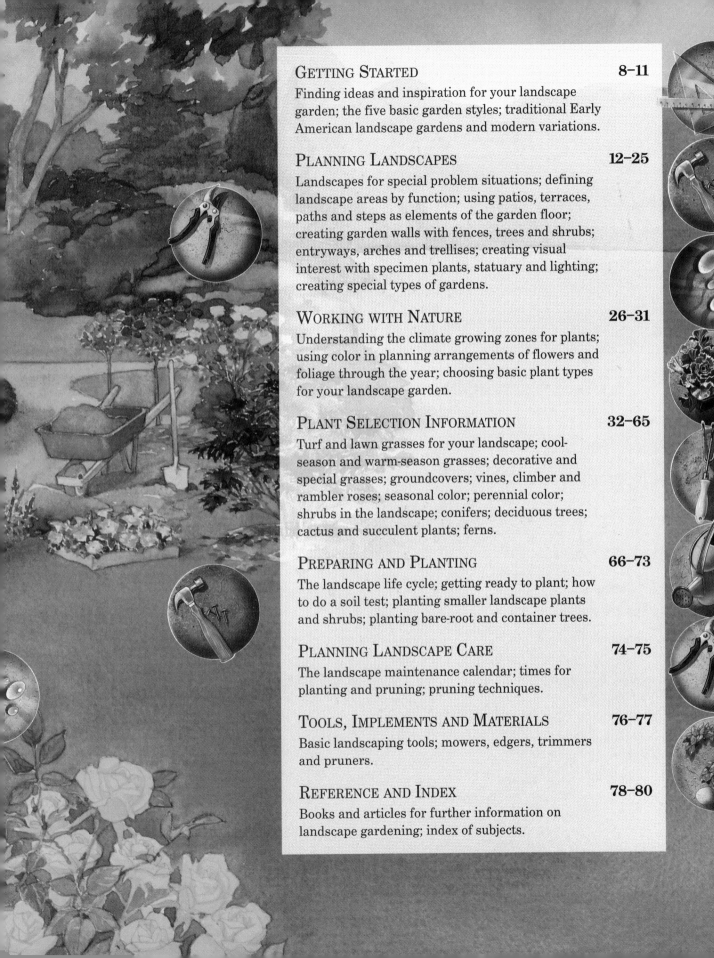

COMPARING LANDSCAPES

Landscape ideas and designs can be found in garden magazines, coffee-table books or even in the paintings of landscape artists. Viewing public and private gardens in your own area, and consulting with landscaping professionals, will help you choose the landscape plan that is best for you.

Natural—
native plants in planned settings

Formal Style—
geometric and orderly

Oriental—
need most care and strict design

Spanish and Moorish — repeating patterns.

Country Garden — careful planning makes an informal look.

BASIC GARDEN STYLES

Planning a landscape garden begins with gathering ideas and insights from every source of garden designs, then working up a plan that includes the elements you wish to use in your site. Sitting down to draw up a garden plan may seem too much like homework, especially if you enjoy just putting plants out, but you will obtain more satisfying results if you design your landscape carefully. Every tree, shrub and plant has a unique color, shape, volume, texture and size; successful landscapes combine them into a pleasing and harmonious design.

You can draw inspiration from the five basic styles that garden planners around the world have developed over the years. The *Formal* Italian or French garden is regular and geometric, with every plant, tree and shrub fitted into an orderly, structured design. The *English* or country garden is a more informal style, but it requires a well-thought-out arrangement of massed shrubs, bunched flowers, and gently curving lines to create an unplanned, natural appearance. *Oriental* gardens rely upon the careful placement of trees, plants, water and stones to develop evocative themes for the viewer's enjoyment; the best Japanese and East Asian gardens skillfully balance informal, natural elements with subtle, asymmetrical patterns that avoid repetition or predictability. In contrast, *Islamic* courtyard gardens display the Moorish-Spanish tradition of repeated geometric patterns, pastel colors and shading to provide relief from harsh sunlight, usually incorporating fountains or pools into the plan. *Native* or low-maintenance natural gardens try to use only naturally-occurring plants and existing topography to create the effect of wildness in a garden setting.

TRADITIONAL LANDSCAPES

The familiar image of the traditional colonial American house and garden brings to mind New England or the Old South, but many of the basic elements of this landscape style can be adapted successfully to any location. Use traditional garden features to develop themes appropriate to the contemporary landscape.

Brick and gravel path

White picket fence

Shade tree

Low hedge

THE TRADITIONAL APPROACH

Early American or colonial-style houses featured both functional and decorative gardens arranged in formal, symmetrical patterns around the residence. Typically, an ornamental "parterre" garden in a formal pattern was bordered by low hedges, enclosing ornamental flower beds or small shaped shrubs within a geometrical brick or gravel walkway. The herb garden near the kitchen and the fruit orchard to the side or rear of the house were set off from the ornamental garden. The traditional white picket fence faced the road and divided the main areas of the gardens.

This formal colonial style gave way to a more informal style, introducing natural elements of the country garden to the domestic landscape. Well-groomed lawns, massed flowers and shrubs set in planting beds along gravel paths, and large shade trees were added to the traditional garden. The white picket fence defined the borders of the garden, the walkways and the property as a whole.

Today, these are still in use in many parts of the country. The colonial style of architecture remains very popular throughout the eastern United States. The landscaper working in this style can draw upon traditional features by using antique garden furniture, flower borders and traditional plants such as boxwood, privet, honeysuckle and periwinkle. Although few landscapers today would choose a parterre garden with white picket fences unless it blended well with the local architecture, landscape elements from more recent periods are often mixed with colonial themes. The cottage garden of the Victorian era, the herb garden of the colonial period and the formal garden of the European tradition can all be used as sources for gardens with traditional themes.

LANDSCAPES FOR SPECIAL SITUATIONS

Not all yards and landscapes are well-suited to the traditional front and side yard arrangement. If you have little or no lawn area, a hilly terrain, or need space for a swimming pool or for children at play, you will have to adapt your landscape plan to fit these conditions.

Shallow Front Yard
If you don't have a yard facing the street, concentrate on landscaping your rear garden or courtyard to take maximum advantage of available space.

Hillside Yard
Landscaping a hillside lot can require careful use of terracing, retaining walls, and other structures, or it may simply call for a spreading groundcover.

12

Play Yard
Play areas should have childproof plants without sharp branches or leaves; chipped bark or heavy-wear grasses make durable and attractive surfaces for playing children.

Pool Landscape
Creative use of plants and shrubs will enable you to design your pool area for privacy and safety, and can help to hide unsightly pool pumps and other equipment.

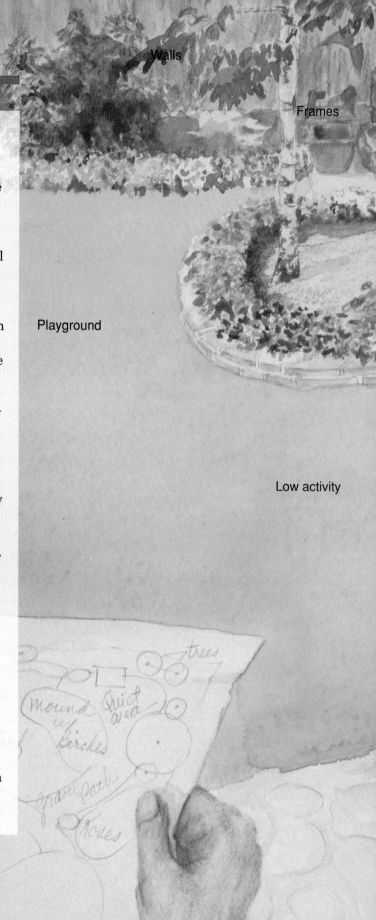

DEFINING AREAS

THINKING ABOUT LANDSCAPES

Drawing a landscape plan to fit your lifestyle involves much more than deciding which plants you want. Take the following into account: houses, driveways, work and play areas, neighboring properties and the special demands imposed by swimming pools, ball courts, and decks or terraces. A landscape only becomes usable when it can be appreciated by walking through, sitting down and looking at it in comfort. All areas should be designed for the active enjoyment of those who will actually use the garden.

Different areas of the landscape receive different amounts of use, of course. Begin by defining different areas of the garden in terms of access points, activities and functional purposes. Then you'll know which spots will receive heavier use, and which can be reserved for decorative elements and view points. Area planning means drawing a measured overhead plan showing the location of all structures, fences, walls, trees, shrubs, paths and steps, then taking photographs from each entry point and view area to help visualize the final effect after planting.

Plan your landscape garden in three dimensions. Try sketching eye-level views from the most-used areas, working from your photographs. Remember that the size of the trees and shrubs will change as they mature, altering the scale and balance of your plantings with respect to each other and to the structures around them. Design your garden for optimum visibility from the garden floor and the house, and for privacy and seclusion from neighboring houses and yards.

Walls

Frames

Playground

Low activity

Occasional
activity

Garden
viewing

Floor

Frequent activity

15

PATIOS, TERRACES, PATHS AND STEPS

When planning the landscape, keep in mind the many options for paving its "floors"—brick, stone, concrete, wood, chips and gravel. Each has its own distinctive texture and form, and each is best suited for a particular need. Choose materials for their use as well as for appearance—non-skid surfaces for safety in wet areas; chipped bark or wood chips to soften play areas; durable stone, brick or concrete for areas that will receive heavy traffic. Always grade and level walkways carefully to prevent hazard from uneven surfaces. Installing proper drainage will insure that any surface water runs off without puddling.

Smooth Textures
Choose brick, marble, tile, concrete or wood for a flat, low-maintenance surface.

Rough Textures
Provide variety with crushed gravel, river pebbles, cobblestones, chips or fieldstones.

ENTERING THE LANDSCAPE

Entryways and walkways define our views of the landscape, so they should be designed to make the best possible impression. Entries and paths also provide access to different areas of the garden for everyday maintenance. Stepping stones and walkways should be made of stable, non-skid materials for sure footing. Brick, pea-gravel, and shredded bark all create attractive textures and patterns for the garden floor.

The purpose of the garden path is to allow one or two persons to walk through in comfort, so pathways should be at least 3 ft. wide—4–5 ft. for two people to walk side-by-side. Remember to leave a buffer area along the side of the path where hedges, tree limbs or shrubs protrude.

The garden path should rarely be straight and narrow; varying the curve and width of the walkway creates a greater variety of perspectives. Gently curving paths can level out steeper climbs and present new, unexpected views of the garden. Sharp intersections and tight curves will feel uncomfortable, just like sharp rocks and unstable surfaces. Flower borders and hedges provide a sense of security where the pedestrian's footing is unsure.

Where the pathway cannot be conveniently curved to go around a slope, use wooden, stone or brick steps to adjust the level of the path to the new height. Steps should come in uniform series, with risers of 4–6 in. and treads of 12–18 in. (3 to 1 ratio). Make the steps wider than the path, and give the treads a slight forward slope for drainage. For shallower grades, use longer ramps with timber risers and earthen treads; steeper steps may require landings or handrails.

Like walkways, steps and stairways benefit from decorative borders. An attractively bordered set of weathered flagstone or timber steps can be a decorative feature in its own right.

Pathways
Winding garden paths suggest other vistas and expand space.

Changing Levels
Steps leading up or down provide easy access and help define uses.

WALLS, FENCES, TREES AND SHRUBS

Garden walls define the boundaries of the landscape, but they also serve many functional and decorative purposes. Use fences or walls as supports and backdrops for greenery that will screen and shade the garden interior. These structures will connect and unify plantings throughout the garden.

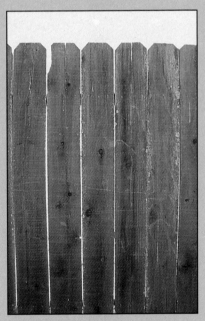

Walls
Low- or medium-height walls can serve as borders, structural supports and retaining barriers; they can also be used as seats or freestanding elements in the garden. Whether using brick, timber, or mortared or dry stone, make sure the wall has solid footings and good drainage.

Fences
Solid wood fences offer security and create boundaries; open and semitransparent fences can also be used for pool barriers, planting barriers and decorative screens. Gates and screens should be made in a style and material suited to the design of the garden areas they enclose.

OUTDOOR SPACES

Think of your garden as an outdoor room with walls made of living plants. The trees provide protection from the wind as well as shade from the sun. Closely planted evergreens, such as spruces, grow together into a solid screen for privacy; shrubs form low hedges and borders. Fast-growing vines climb over fences to create walls of foliage. Decorative plants, fences and structures all help create a sense of interior space.

Landscape trees and shrubs come in a wide variety of shapes and sizes, but they can be thought of in terms of their basic forms. Vertical trees, such as the Italian cypress, are upright pillars. Rounded trees spread their branches out into spheres. Many conifers form pyramidal shapes, but some branch out into irregular horizontal forms. Shrubs also come in all varieties of upright, conical, rounded and horizontal shapes. Placed in a balanced, rhythmic landscape composition, trees and shrubs will lend variety to the simplest outdoor space.

The outdoor room has a much higher ceiling and larger floor space than a small interior room, so you should place your trees and shrubs with a feeling for the scale of the landscape. Smaller plants and shrubs belong in the foreground, while larger shrubs and trees should form the background, to create a sense of distance and perspective that feels natural for the size of your garden.

Trees and Shrubs
To create natural barriers and define the visual space of the garden, trees and shrubs can be planted in regular patterns around the perimeter of the garden. This wall of trees will enhance privacy and create a foliage backdrop for smaller garden plants.

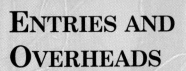

ENTRIES AND OVERHEADS

The entry to the landscape garden should welcome the visitor, either through the formal design of a gate, door or archway, or through the informal arrangement of a trellis or plant-covered arch. Breaks in walls, screens and hedges also create inviting transitions between garden areas.

Overhead Structures
Overhead structures provide seasonal shade for central areas of the landscape. Climbing vines and shrubs lend an ornamental touch to the structures.

Tree Canopies
Mature trees provide shade and shelter, filtering the sun and creating varied patterns of light and dark.

CREATING
VISUAL ELEMENTS

Individual plants, garden fixtures and structures should be placed where they will create the most visual interest in the garden. Four ways you can engage the viewer's eye in the landscape include topiary and espalier, garden lighting, sculptures and fountains, and rare and unusual specimen plants.

SPECIMEN PLANTS
Unusual or distinctive plants can serve either as focal points or as eye-catching accents.

Topiary and Espalier
Create living designs by training plants on a framework of wood or wire set against a wall or fence to outline its form.

Topiary plants are trained and pruned into ornamental figures.

Lighting
Nighttime viewing of your landscape garden can be dramatically enhanced with accent lighting.

Statues, fountains and sculptures
Statuary can provide dramatic emphasis of a garden theme. Bring moving water into the garden, whether in a fountain, waterfall or stream.

SPECIAL GARDENS IN THE LANDSCAPE

Special "gardens within gardens" draw attention by mood, form and pattern, or clusters of color. For example, Japanese gardens are places of peaceful tranquility and rock gardens catch your eye. Shady nooks, with plants that prefer indirect sunlight, relieve the soul with their coolness and quiet.

Landscape Flower Border
The English flower border is a tradition for both country and cottage gardens, creating natural edgings with masses of color and a variety of plants.

FORMAL ROSE GARDEN
A raised bed of roses can be a feature within the landscape, or a special garden unto itself. Provide ample footpaths and access points for close-up viewing of the roses.

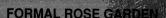

Hillside Features
Create berms and small hills to separate planting areas and to enclose flower beds of seasonal color.

Groves and Miniature Forests
By clustering plantings of specimen trees and shrubs, you can create the effect of a woodland grove or miniature forest in a small area.

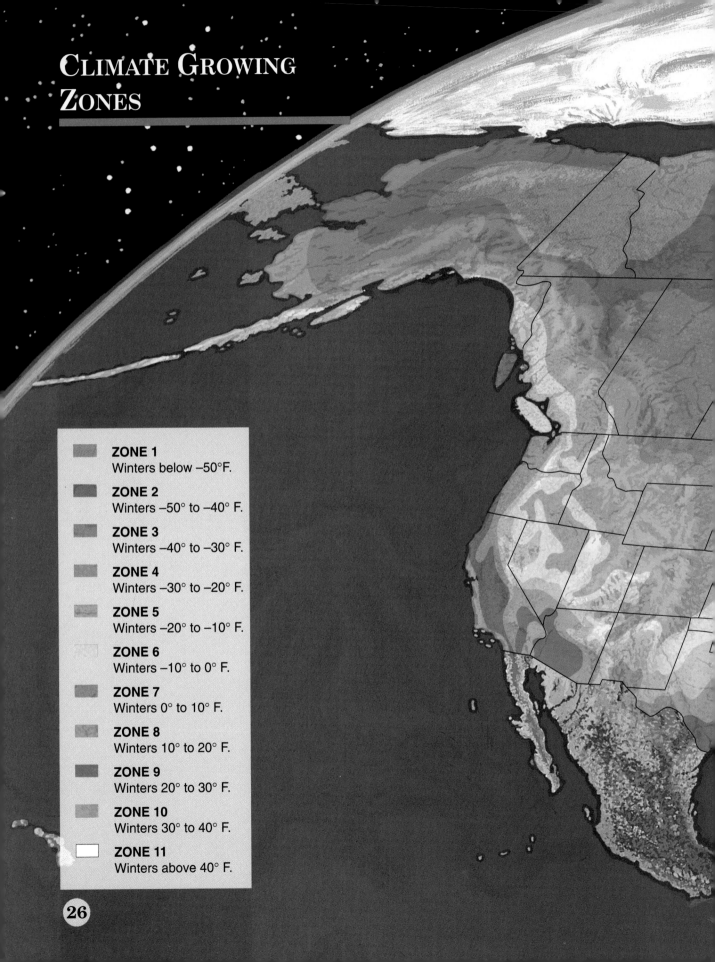

Climate Growing Zones

ZONE 1
Winters below −50°F.

ZONE 2
Winters −50° to −40° F.

ZONE 3
Winters −40° to −30° F.

ZONE 4
Winters −30° to −20° F.

ZONE 5
Winters −20° to −10° F.

ZONE 6
Winters −10° to 0° F.

ZONE 7
Winters 0° to 10° F.

ZONE 8
Winters 10° to 20° F.

ZONE 9
Winters 20° to 30° F.

ZONE 10
Winters 30° to 40° F.

ZONE 11
Winters above 40° F.

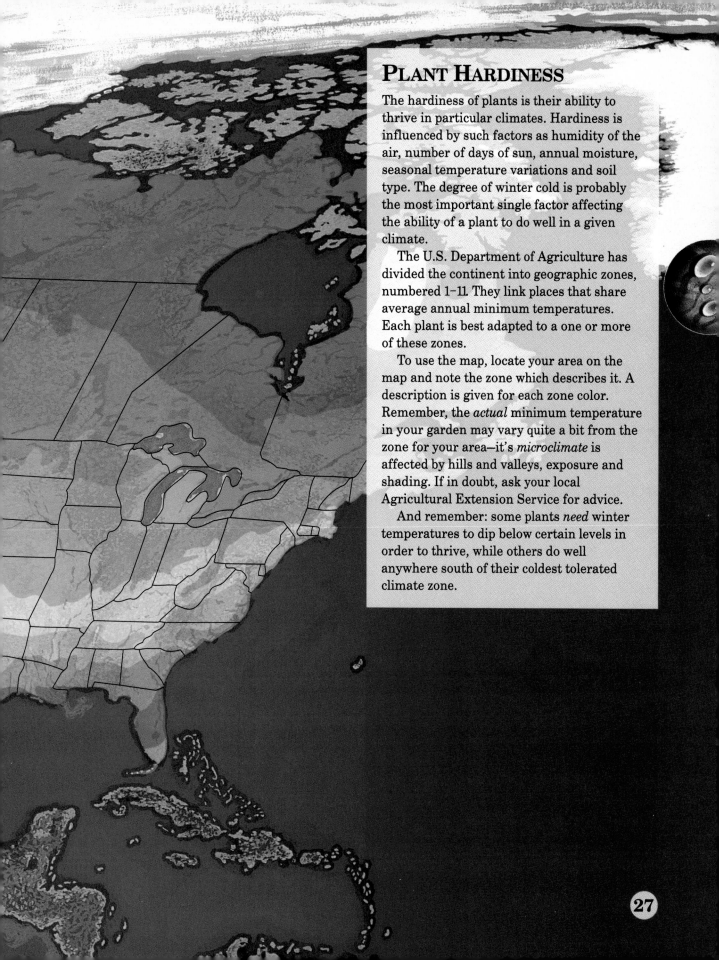

PLANT HARDINESS

The hardiness of plants is their ability to thrive in particular climates. Hardiness is influenced by such factors as humidity of the air, number of days of sun, annual moisture, seasonal temperature variations and soil type. The degree of winter cold is probably the most important single factor affecting the ability of a plant to do well in a given climate.

The U.S. Department of Agriculture has divided the continent into geographic zones, numbered 1–11. They link places that share average annual minimum temperatures. Each plant is best adapted to a one or more of these zones.

To use the map, locate your area on the map and note the zone which describes it. A description is given for each zone color. Remember, the *actual* minimum temperature in your garden may vary quite a bit from the zone for your area—it's *microclimate* is affected by hills and valleys, exposure and shading. If in doubt, ask your local Agricultural Extension Service for advice.

And remember: some plants *need* winter temperatures to dip below certain levels in order to thrive, while others do well anywhere south of their coldest tolerated climate zone.

COLOR IN THE GARDEN

Yellows

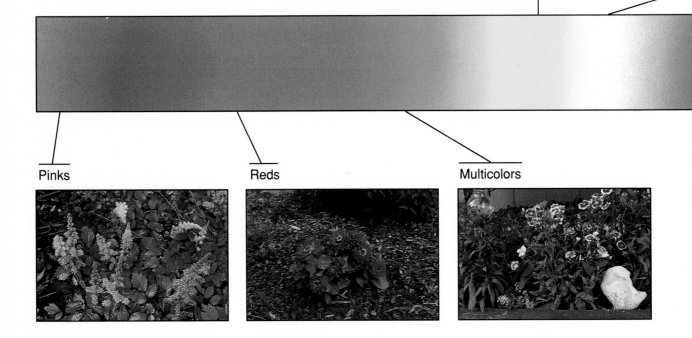

Pinks

Reds

Multicolors

Foliage Color
Choose foliage plantings to emphasize or subdue
nearby annuals, perennials and bulb plantings.

Whites

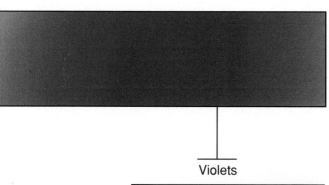

Violets

Seasonal Color
Create striking garden accents with color spots;
some will bloom in autumn, others in spring or
summer. Colorful bark creates winter interest.

CHOOSING GARDEN COLOR

Gardeners use color in their gardens as artists use paint from their palettes. Color can be found anywhere in the garden: tree bark, foliage, flowers, turf, bricks, stones or structures. Take care to choose only those colors that you wish to see, and to use them in ways that work together as the seasons change.

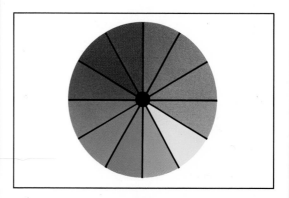

The color wheel will help you choose between the bright, primary colors—red, yellow and blue—and their softer complements—green, purple and orange. Hues opposite each other on the color wheel match appealingly, while those that are closer together clash with eye-dazzling contrast. Cool colors such as green and blue are more restful and appear to recede from the warmer, livelier colors—red, yellow, pink and orange.

Use these chromatic combinations in selecting garden colors. Choose a quiet, cool background of evergreen shrubs to emphasize bright red and yellow spring flowers. By the time nearby color-packed foliage trees turn, these flowers will be gone, but green foliage will still be there, making a maple tree's display of fall color all the more eye-catching. Even in winter, evergreen shrubs and hollies provide a deep green backdrop for bare branches and snow.

By matching and contrasting the colors of flower and foliage, you can create a sequence of visual backgrounds and accents that changes continuously throughout the year.

29

LANDSCAPE PLANT GROUPS

In the pages that follow, you will find the basic landscape plant groups, each with a list of selected types and species suitable to your gardening needs. Check out the individual species for their growth habits, frost hardiness, soil preference and any special requirements for fertilizing and watering.

Turf and Lawn Grasses—Pgs. 32–37
Cool and warm season lawn grasses suitable for your area; decorative clumping grasses and extra-hardy grasses for problem areas.

Vines and Climber Roses—Pgs. 42–45
Different varieties of clinging tendril and climbing vines; training vines on walls, trellises and fences; climber and rambler roses.

Groundcovers—Pgs. 38–41
Deciduous and evergreen groundcovers for every landscaping situation; tips on installation and maintenance for different species.

Seasonal and Perennial Color—Pgs. 46–49
Annual, biennial and perennial plants for garden color throughout the growing season; choosing between nursery grown annuals and perennials.

Shrubs—Pgs. 50–55
Using evergreen and deciduous shrubs in the landscape; selecting shrubs for size, shape and color; feeding, shaping and pruning your shrubs.

Cactus and Succulents—Pgs. 62–63
Creating arid country landscapes with cactus and succulents; the basics of cactus and succulent care; using ice plant for flowering groundcover.

Trees—Pgs. 56–61
Characteristics of fine-needled conifers and broadleafed evergreen and deciduous trees; ornamental, shade and screen trees suitable for your area.

Ferns—Pgs. 64–65
Using woodland ferns in the landscape; soil, sun and water requirements of the most popular ferns.

CHOOSING GRASSES

Whether you're installing turf for the first time or renovating an established lawn, careful planning and ground preparation are essential. Many grasses are sensitive to extremes of temperature and rainfall, so select appropriate grasses.

Lawn grasses are generally divided into cool-season and warm-season species; local variations in rainfall, soil type and sun or shade will determine the best species for you. Most varieties are available as seed or sod, but some of the warm-season grasses, such as St. Augustine and Improved Bermuda, are also sold as sprigs or plugs. Seeds are available as straight and blended species, or as mixes developed for optimum pest and disease resistance in particular areas. Seeding is inexpensive but can involve watering and considerable maintenance until the lawn is established.

Also decide how much maintenance you want to do—lawns require regular watering, fertilizing and mowing. Every type of grass has different requirements for mowing height, pest control and soil nutrition. Low maintenance lawns using native grasses and groundcovers are increasingly popular, but special decorative grasses can also be used to create variety and color accents within the landscape.

Don't be frightened off. Turfgrasses require regular care and upkeep, but can be easy to maintain.

Colonial Bentgrass

Agrostis tenuis

Fine-leaved cool-season grass. Browns easily; heavy watering. Mow to 1/4–1 in. Seed, sprig or sod.

Creeping Bentgrass

Agrostis palustris

Ideal for putting greens; requires low mowing and sandy loam. Poor drought and disease tolerance. Mow to 1/4–1 in. Seed, sprig or sod.

Kentucky Bluegrass

Poa pratensis

Excellent dark green lawn grass. Steady watering, moderate feeding. Mow to 1 1/2–2 in. Seed, sprig or sod.

Hard or Sheep's Fescue

Festuca ovina

Grows and wears well in hot weather or shade. Disease resistant. Requires little water. Mow 1 1/2 in. high. Seed in fall or spring.

Red Fescue

Festuca rubra

Does well in shade, dry soil. Tolerates acid soil. Mow to 2–3 in. Seed, sprig or sod.

Annual Ryegrass

Lolium multiflorum

Not recommended. Medium- to coarse-leaved annual grass; tends to clump. Heavy watering. Mow to 1 1/2–2 in. Seed or sprig.

Chewings Fescue

Festuca rubra 'commutata'

Shade tolerant, dry soil. Mixes well with Kentucky bluegrass. Mow to 1–2 in. Seed or sprig.

Tall Fescue

Festuca arundinacea

Drought tolerant coarse fescue. Excellent for lawns. Tolerates part shade. Mow to 3–4 in. Seed or sprig.

Perennial Ryegrass

Lolium perenne

Coarse, drought tolerant grass. Likes mild winters, cool summers. Mow to 1–2 in. Seed, sprig or sod.

Bahiagrass

Paspalum notatum

Coarse, fast-growth and easy-care grass. Tolerates shade and drought. Mow to 2–3 in., moderate fertilization. Seed.

Improved Bermudagrass

Cynodon dactylon

Better appearance and performance than common bermudagrass. Mow to 1/2–1 in. Sprigs, plugs or sod.

Common Bermudagrass

Cynodon dactylon

Drought tolerant; needs full sun. Heavy fertilization, mow to 1 in. Sprigs, plugs, sod or seed.

Buffalograss

Buchloe dactyloides

Thin, drought-tolerant grass used in high plains from Texas to Canada; mow to 1 in., browns in winter. Sprigs, plugs or sod.

Centipedegrass

Eremochloa ophiuroides

Hardy, easy-care grass. Tolerates light shade and poor soil. Mow to 2 in. Sprigs, plugs, sod or seed.

Saltgrass

Puccinellia distans 'fults'

Tolerates saline, alkaline soil where other turfgrasses cannot grow. Seed or sd.

Seashore Paspalum

Paspalum vaginatum

Cool coastal area grass; full sun, drought tolerant. Sold in spring as sod. Mow to 2 in.

Zoysiagrass

Zoysia japonica

Fine textured warm climate grass, often sold as plugs. Slow growing; mow to 1/2–1 1/2 in. Sprigs, plugs or sod.

St. Augustinegrass

Stenotaphrum secundatum

Good shade grass, tolerates salty soil. Heavy watering, mow to 1 1/2–2 1/2 in. Sprigs, plugs or sod.

Decorative and Special Grasses

Reedgrass

Calamagrostis x acutiflora

Tall annual-flowering hybrid reed grass. Full or part sun, damp soil. Zones 3–9.

Blue Fescue

Festuca ovina glauca

Mounds of blue-gray leaves 6–12 in. Good for borders and accents. Zones 4–10.

Fountaingrass

Pennisetum alopecuroides

Dark green decorative grass, grows to 3–4 ft. Foxtail flower spikes. Full sun, well-drained soil. Zones 6–9.

Blue Oatgrass

Helictotrichon sempervirens

Blue-gray clumping grass, grows to 3–4 ft. Needs sun, well-drained soil. Zones 4–8.

Pampasgrass

Cortaderia selloana

Large (8–12 ft.) plumed grass, long arching leaves 2–3 ft., cream-colored plumes to 20 ft. High maintenance; full sun, rich well-drained sandy soil. Zones 8–10, further north as annual.

Mondograss

Ophiopogon japonicus

Slow-growing evergreen grass, to 6 in. or higher. Spreads by runners, forms sod. Full or part shade, full shade in hot climates. Pale purple summer flowers. Zones 8–10.

Sea Pink

Armeria maritima

Small clumping plant, pink flowers in late spring, summer. 6-in. leaves, stems to 1 ft. or more. Fast growing. Zones 4–9.

Stipa

Stipa species

Fine-stemmed feathery grass grows to 3 ft. Full sun, well-drained soil. Zones 5–9.

GROUNDCOVERS

PLANTING GROUNDCOVERS

For landscapes where turfgrass lawns and flower beds are difficult—hillsides, rocky surfaces, under trees and in overly dry or wet soil—groundcovers are an excellent, low-maintenance alternative. Groundcovers can be almost any durable, low-growing plant that spreads horizontally to form a carpet-like surface; they knit their roots into soil, spread over brick and stone into crevices, and even creep around barriers and borders. Once well established, groundcovers generally require little upkeep.

Groundcovers have a number of important roles in the garden—erosion control, foliage and flower color, weed control and edging. Put them to good use. As a rule, groundcovers should be planted in the spring. Limit access until they are well established. Different groundcover species adapt to most conditions, but good drainage is desirable.

Although groundcovers need less maintenance, they require special care during installation. Select a type suitable to your landscape and buy enough plants to cover the entire area. Loosen the soil to 4–6 in. and check that each plant has a strong root system. Groundcover will spread its vines or send out runners to intertwine with its neighbors in short order.

Until they are established, most groundcovers will need regular watering and fertilization.

Carpet Bugle

Ajuga reptans

Fast-growing perennial, to 12 in. Deep blue or white flowers in late spring. Subject to disease. Zones 2–3.

Bearberry, Kinnikinnick

Arctostaphylos uva-ursi

Medium-fast growth to 1 ft. high, spreads to 15 ft. White and pink flowers in early spring, berries in summer. Sun to part shade. Zones 3–7.

Silver Lace

Artemisia species

Perennial herb, 1–3 ft. tall, with silver leaves and small flowers. Drought resistant and salt tolerant. Plant in well-drained soil and full sun. Zones 3–9.

Plumbago

Ceratostigma plumbaginoides

Nearly evergreen, low mat to 18 in. Blue flowers in summer, fall. Foliage colors with frost. Well-drained, fertile soil. Zones 5–9.

Rock Cotoneaster

Cotoneaster horizontalis

Medium-fast growth to 3 ft. Pink-white flowers, dark green, herringbone-pattern leaves. Full sun. Zones 4–7.

Dichondra

Dichondra repens caroliniensis

Fast-growing evergreen, up to 1 ft. Low, round-leaf groundcover that tolerates shade. Mow to 1 in. Low maintenance but heavy fertilization. Zones 9–10.

Winter Creeper

Euonymus fortunei

Hardy evergreen vine, trails out to 20 ft. Leaves turn purple in autumn and winter. Zones 4–9.

Ivy

Hedera species

Medium-growth, dark green 2–3-in. leaves spread by aerial roots. Moist soil, sun or shade. Zones 5–10.

Plantation Lily

Hosta species

Mounding, slow growth to 3 ft. Spike-like lavender to pink bloom in late summer. Part sun or shade, moist soil. Zones 3–9.

GROUNDCOVERS

Aaron's Beard

Hypericum calycinum

Fast-growing evergreen, up to 1 ft. high. Yellow flowers in late spring, early summer. Sun or shade. Zones 5–8.

Isotoma

Isotoma species

Dainty small leaves of light green and tiny, star-shaped flowers in white, blue or purple, to 1 ft. Zones 8–10.

Trailing Lantana

Lantana montevidensis

Fast-growing evergreen, to 3 ft. high, spreads to 6 ft. Low maintenance. Full sun, little watering. Zones 8–10.

Creeping Lilyturf

Liriope species

Evergreen leaves, medium growth to 10 in. Clumps merge by spreading underground runners. Full or part sun. Zones 6–10.

Oregon Grape

Mahonia repens

Thornless evergreen, 3-in. leaves, blue-black berries in fall. Sun to part shade, moderate watering. Zones 5–10.

Japanese Spurge

Pachysandra terminalis

Moderate-growth green foliage evergreen, to 5–10 in. high. Does well in shade, needs regular watering and acid soil. Zones 3–8.

Moss Phlox

Phlox subulata

Matting perennial with semievergreen, needle-like foliage to 6 in. Pink flowers in spring. Sun, well-drained soil. Zones 2–3.

Santolina

Santolina chamaecyparissus

Gray foliage evergreen, medium-growth to 2 ft. high, spreads up to 6 ft. Drought tolerant, small yellow flowers in spring. Zones 7–8.

Cinquefoil

Potentilla species

Fast-growing evergreen, to 6 in. high. Sun to part shade in hot climates. Zones 2–8.

Sedum

Sedum species

Slow-growing succulent, to 2 in. Yellow flowers in late spring. Full sun, moderate watering. Zones 4–9.

Rosemary

Rosmarinus officinalis

Medium-fast-growing evergreen, to 2–4 ft high. Fragrant, dark green needles. Blue flowers in early spring. Full sun, well-drained soil. Zones 7–10 East.

Dwarf Periwinkle

Vinca minor

Fast-growing, hardy trailing evergreen, 2-in. leaves. Blue flowers in spring. Full or part shade, well-drained soil. Zones 5–9.

41

VINES

CLIMBING VINES

Vines are one of the most varied and useful plant groups available to the landscape gardener. They can be trained to climb up vertical supports or across arbors and trellises, to cover fences and walls or to create screens providing shade from the sun. There are numerous varieties of foliage, flowering and fruit-bearing vines.

Vining plants are any species of plant that grows by elongating its stems so as to climb vertically or creep horizontally. Vines can climb by a number of methods, from trailing out stems or hooking onto supports with thorns or spikes, to weaving in and out of whatever object presents itself. Some vines set out roots which anchor them onto rocks, branches and trunks, or any surface with holes or cracks. Most vines either twine themselves, clockwise or counter-clockwise, with a slow rotary movement of the growing tip of the stem, or cling with tendrils or stickers that grip or coil around supporting surfaces.

Most vines are warm-weather plants, but some are hardy enough for northern climates. To choose a vine for your landscape, first consider how and where it will climb or creep as it grows—horizontally as a groundcover, or up a trellis as a screen. Vines can be attractive for their foliage alone (ivy), for their flowers (clematis), or for their scent (honeysuckle). Most vines are fairly vigorous and fast-growing plants, but some require special care. A few can be real troublemakers unless they are diligently pruned. One such problem vine, the notorious kudzu (*Pueraria lobata*), grows from 50–75 ft. a year in the moist, hot areas of the Deep South, covering everything in sight.

Clematis

Clematis species

Fast-growing, deciduous vine, to 10–12 ft. high. Blue-purple flowers are 4–6 in. wide, bloom summer and fall. Dies to ground in cold winters. Part shade; moist, well-drained soil. Zones 5–9.

Honeysuckle

Lonicera species

Fast-growing, hardy vine, train to 10–15 ft. Red, 2-in. flowers in summer. Full sun or part shade, moist but well-drained soil. Zones 5–10.

Bougainvillea

Bougainvillea species

Vertically-climbing by twining stems and thorns, brilliant purple, red, orange or white flowers peak in summer. Full sun, moist soil. Zone 10.

Wine Grape

Vitus vinifera

Deciduous vine with dominant trunk and branch pattern for winter interest. Grows to 50 ft. Vigorous and hardy. Zones 5–10.

Wisteria

Wisteria species

Hardy, grows up to 50 ft. high. Strong, woody trunks need good support. Full sun, well-drained soil; shelter from wind. Zones 3–10.

Boston Ivy

Parthenocissus tricuspidata

Highly popular ivy of "Ivy League" to 50 ft. Semi-evergreen. Good fall color, fast grower. Well-drained soil. Zones 5–10.

Passionflower

Passiflora species

Fast-spreading, grows to 20 ft. or more. Good for trellises; showy 3–4 in. flowers. Moist, well-drained sandy loam. Zone 10.

Star Jasmine

Trachelospermum jasminoides

Slow-growing evergreen, twining to 15–20 ft. or more. Fragrant, yellow-white flowers in spring and summer. Moist, well-drained soil; part shade. Zones 9–10.

CLIMBER AND RAMBLER ROSES

ROSES IN THE LANDSCAPE

Among ornamental plants, roses are usually thought of as flowering shrubs. They are admired chiefly for their color and fragrance. Roses known as climbers and ramblers can also provide vertical foliage and background color, cover fences, or spread horizontally as a sturdy groundcover.

Most of the so-called climbing roses don't actually cling or grasp to their vertical supports. They need to be trained and tied in order to climb upward on trellises, arbors and fences. True rambler roses, on the other hand, will follow any solid support—train them along arbors, pillars and posts. They make a lovely cover for landscape structures, twining their thorny canes into and around arches and gazebos, gradually assuming their shape.

Many climbing roses bloom only once a season, but also serve as year-round foliage, hedges or groundcovers—their seasonal color is an added bonus.

Rambler roses generally have smaller, clustering flowers—prune them only to remove diseased or damaged canes. Then cut again after blooming is finished for a good color show the following year. Climbers, on the other hand, bloom with larger flowers, once or twice a season, depending on the cultivar type. Prune one-time flowering types after they bloom in the spring, or just before winter dormancy ends for the multiple bloomers.

Climbing America

Warriner, 1976

Well-formed, large, coral-pink blooms. Flowers have rich, spicy scent and form on new and old wood. Long canes. AARS 1976.

Climbing Pinata 3996

Suzuki, 1978

Bright yellow and orange-red blooms. Canes grow 6–8 ft. high.

Climbing Blaze

Kallay, 1932

Most popular climber. Masses of bright red blooms in large clusters form on new and old wood.

Climbing White Dawn

Longley, 1949

Constant blooms of clear white, ruffled flowers on a vigorous, disease-resistant plant. Blooms on new and old wood.

Climbing High Noon

Lammerts, 1948

Lemon yellow, large, fragrant flowers set off by shiny green foliage. Disease resistant. Blooms on new and old wood. AARS 1948.

Climbing Joseph's Coat

Swim & Armstrong, 1964

Very popular multicolor climber in shades of pink, red, orange and yellow. Blooms on new and old wood.

Climbing Blue Girl

Kordes, 1964

Sport of parent Blue Girl. Large, fragrant lavender flowers. Vigorous. Blooms on new and old wood.

Climbing Golden Showers

Lammerts, 1956

Masses of fragrant, pure yellow, ruffled flowers. Good climber. Blooms on new and old wood. AARS 1956.

Climbing Royal Gold

Morey, 1957

Deep yellow "Hybrid Tea" blooms with stems long enough to cut. Fragrant. Blooms on new and old wood.

Climbing Don Juan

Maladrone, 1958

Deep, velvety red, 5 in. flowers. Vigorous, very fragrant. Blooms on new and old wood.

Tempo 3652

Warriner, 1975

Bright red flower clusters cover from spring to fall. Bright, dark green foliage. Blooms on new and old wood.

Seasonal Color

Container-Grown Bedding Plants

When purchasing container-grown plants, you will be choosing between annual, biennial and perennial plants. Annuals are grown from seed, and complete their life cycle within a single growing season. Biennials are also grown from seed one year to flower in the next. Sow your annuals from seed or buy container-grown plants. They are sold in packs, small pots or flats that permit quick and easy installation of flowering borders and beds and allow the composition of color sequences, by moving the pots around before planting.

Perennials are long-term landscaping plants. They return, year after year, to bloom again in the growing season. Once large enough, many can be divided again and again. Most perennials are used in combination with annuals and bulbs to create a continuing, season-long sequence of color in the garden.

Shrubs and trees should also be considered for their seasonal color; note their order of bloom and whether their foliage turns with the seasons when planning the color sequence of the landscape plants around your flower beds. Contrast planting brings out the best in plant color, form and texture, no matter which seasonal color plants you are considering.

Cosmos

Cosmos species

Annual from 4–6 ft. in height, making excellent borders and massed plantings. 1–2 in. flowers from white to yellow-gold to pink. Full sun, dry soil.

Coleus

Coleus species

Varigated foliage ranging from green to white and red. Sun to full shade, moist location.

Marigold

Tagetes species

Bright, ruffled flowers on short or tall stalks bloom until frost. Full sun.

Periwinkle

Vinca species

Low, vining growth to 10 in. White or pink flowers in spring and summer. Full sun or part shade in moist soil.

Impatiens

Impatiens species

Dark green leaves; grows to 1–2 ft. with 2–3 in. flowers in wide variety of colors. Rich, moist soil, full or part shade.

Sage

Salvia speciies

Grows from 1–2 ft. high. Bright flower spikes atop attractive leaves. Full sun or part shade.

Sweet Alyssum

Lobularia maritima

Mounding edge plant with white, pink or lavender flowers in summer. Full sun.

Petunia

Petunia x hybrida

Varieties grow from 10–15 in., showing 2–5 in. early blossoms in all colors. Full sun, sandy well-drained soil.

Zinnia

Zinnia elegans

Popular annual, grows to 2–3 ft. with large, 2–6 in. flowers in all colors. Full sun, rich and well-drained soil. Regular watering and feeding.

Begonia

Begonia species

Grows to 1 ft. with widely varied flowers and foliage color from summer to fall. Semi-sunny, moist sites.

Geranium

Pelargonium species

Trailing or upright plant to 18 in. high, clusters of flowers in a wide range of colors. Cool climates only. Slightly acid, well-drained soil. Full sun.

Violets and Pansies

Viola species

Perennial grown as annual; 6–8 in. high. Sun or part shade. Needs moist soil.

PERENNIALS

Yarrow

Achillea filipendula

Native in some areas, tall herb to 3 ft. Flowers in spring and summer. Full sun in damp, humus-rich soil. Zones 3–9.

Spiraea

Astilbe species

White, pink or bright red stalks of feathery flowers in summer. Full to part sun, moist soils. Zones 4–8.

Hollyhock

Alcea rosea

Heritage flowers with tall spikes of blooms in summer to fall, to 6 ft. Full sun in rich soil. Zones 2–9.

Bellflower

Campanula species

Violet flowers from spring to summer, on low plants to 10 in. Full or part sun. Zones 3–9.

Columbine

Aquilegia species

Single or double flowers in spring, with graceful foliage to 2 1/2 ft. Full or part sun. Zones 3–9.

Shasta Daisy

Chrysanthemum maximum

A sunny garden classic—flowers with white radiating petals from a bright yellow center reach 6 in. diameter, to 4 ft. Zones 5–9.

Delphinium

Delphinium species

Stalks to 6 ft. tall, purple 2-in. flowers in summer. Full sun, moist, well-drained soil. Zones 3–10.

Lupine

Lupinus polyphyllus

Tall, with spikes of flowers in blue, pink, red, yellow and purple, to 5 ft. Full sun, sandy soils. Zones 4–7.

Bleeding Heart

Dicentra spectabilis

Native plant to 18 in. tall, with hanging, heart-like flowers from spring to fall. Shady, moist soil. Zones 2–3.

Poppy

Papaver species

Beautiful pastel flowers on tall stalks, to 6 ft. Flowers in spring and summer. Full sun in moist soil. Zones 1–8.

Daylily

Hemerocallis species

Striking trumpets of brightly colored, multiple flowers on tall stalks, to 30 in. Full to part sun, moist soils. Zones 3–9.

Gloriosa Daisy

Rudbeckia hirta

Hybrid of wild Black-eyed Susan, blooms in summer and fall with striking flowers on tall stems, to 24 in. Full sun. Zones 3–9.

SHRUBS

Abelia

Abelia grandiflora

Mounding shrub, grows to 5 ft. or more. Deciduous in northern range. Sun or part shade, well-drained soil. Zones 5–9.

SHRUBS IN THE LANDSCAPE

Long-lasting and versatile, landscape shrubs can be adapted to almost any garden plan. They serve as flowering plants, foliage color, hedges, edgings and even as screens. Shrubs are low-maintenance plants, requiring only occasional pruning and fertilization unless they are being shaped into formal hedges. Their variety is the key to their versatility—nearly every size, shape, color and texture may be found.

Shrub selection should be done in the early stages of landscape planning. Individual flowering or specimen shrubs should be placed as accents in conspicuous spots, while groups of spreading shrubs can be planted closely together to form dense walls of vegetation around the landscape. Depending on their size and type of foliage, shrubs can give a light, airy feeling to the landscape, or add weight and mass as backdrops and screens. Trained as vertical forms, shrubs become treelike—the larger upright shrubs are often indistinguishable from small trees.

Shrubs can be evergreen or deciduous, flowering or foliage only, low-growing, upright or even climbing. Like trees, shrubs should be planted with a view to their final, mature size and shape.

Many shrubs can be bought or grown as dwarf specimens, and frequent pruning will always control a shrub's final size.

Barberry

Berberis thunbergii

Medium-slow growing deciduous shrub; dense, dark green leaves, yellow flowers. Scarlet color, red berries in fall. Sun to part shade, moist well-drained soil. Zones 4–8.

Boxwood

Buxus species

Upright, hardy evergreen for formal plantings, can grow to 3–4 ft. Sun or part shade, takes shearing. Zones 5–9.

Heather

Calluna vulgaris

Small, narrow-leaved evergreen, grows to 2–3 ft. Purple-pink flowers. Moist, acid soil, full sun. Zones 4–6.

Dogwood

Cornus species

Reddish limbs with showy white flowers that appear in early spring, vivid foliage color in fall. Part shade. Zones 2–8.

Camellia

Camellia Japonica

Popular evergreen plant, upright to spreading form. Long dark leaves, brilliant flowers. Shade or part-sun, rich acid soil. Zones 7–8.

Smokebush

Cotinus coggygria

Tall, to 15 ft. or more, with broad, flat leaves and feathery flowers in spring. Good fall color. Full sun. Zones 5–9.

Dwarf Hinoki Cypress

Chamaecyparis obtusa

Small evergreen, needs pruning to keep to 5 ft. or less. Interesting spreading branch forms. Zones 5–9.

Cotoneaster

Cotoneaster species

Deciduous shrub, low-growing to 1 ft. White flowers in summer. Full sun, little care. Zones 4–7.

Shrubs

Daphne

Daphne species

Evergreen vase-shaped shrub, grows to 3 ft. or more. Pink flowers in spring. Needs good, slightly alkaline soil. Zones 4–8.

Euonymus

Euonymus species

High shrub to 12 ft. with glorious fall color foliage. Full to part sun, moist soil. Zones 3–8.

Veronica

Hebe species

Round, low evergreen, grows to 5 ft. Purple, spiking flowers in summer. Full sun, well-drained soil. Zones 8–10.

Hydrangea

Hydrangea species

Medium bush to 5 ft. with large green leaves and masses of flowers in summer. Full to part sun, in moist soil. Zones 4–9.

Holly

Ilex species

Holly grows from 2–20 ft. high. Full sun, part shade. Zones 5–10.

Juniper

Juniper species

Easily trained, low or high shrub with dense, evergreen foliage. Full sun, does well even in poor soils. Zones 3–9.

Myrtle

Myrtus communis

Aromatic leaves. Dense shrub grows to 8–10 ft. White flowers in summer, berries in fall. Full sun, dry soil. Zones 8–9.

Honeysuckle

Lonicera species

Vine-like hedge shrub, with fragrant flowers, to 15 ft. with support. Red or yellow flowers in summer. Sun. Zones 3–9.

Heavenly Bamboo

Nandina domestica

Upright stalks, evergreen, member of Barberry family, grows to 8 ft. Bright red berries, scarlet foliage in autumn. Sun or part shade. Zones 6–9.

Star Magnolia

Magnolia stellata

Upright deciduous shrub or tree to 20 ft. White flowers in spring. Fertile, well-drained soil. Zones 5–9.

SHRUBS

Dwarf Ninebark

Physocarpus opulifolius

Dark green, mounding deciduous shrub, grows from 2–5 ft. Small white to pink flowers. Zones 2–8.

Bird's Nest Spruce

Picea abies 'nidiformis'

Low, dense evergreen, slow-growing to spreading bush. Dwarf form of Norway Spruce. Zones 2–8.

Cinquefoil

Potentilla species

Finely textured foliage with multiple blooms in summer, to 5 ft. Sun in moist soil. Zones 2–8.

Azalea

Rhododendron species

Rounded, spreading deciduous shrub, grows to 4 ft. Part shade, well-drained sandy loam. Zones 4–9.

Rhododendron

Rhododendron species

Dense-leaved native plant, provides tall evergreen backdrop to 25 ft. Flowers in summer. Full or part shade, acid soil. Zones 3–8.

Japanese Rose

Rosa rugosa

Spreading, dark-green deciduous shrub, grows to 6 ft. Pink or white flowers in June, large red hips in fall. Hardy to Zone 2–9.

Spiraea

Speraea species

Graceful arching branches with white flowers, to 6 ft. Full sun in moist soils. Zone 4–8.

Lilac

Syringa species

Fragrant deciduous upright, grows to 20 ft. White or purple flowers in early summer. Full sun, any good soil. Zones 3–8.

Dwarf Yew

Taxus brevifolia

Small, slow-growing evergreen hedge and edging plant, shears well, grows to 4–5 ft. Any well-drained soil. Sun or shade. Zones 4–8.

Germander

Teucrium chamaedrys

Medium-growth evergreen, spreads to 2 ft. or more. Small, deep-purple or white flowers in summer. Full sun or part shade, well-drained soil. Zones 6–8.

Viburnum

Viburnum species

Narrow-leaved evergreen to 8 ft. Deeply-veined leaves. White flowers in fall. Part shade. Zones 4–8.

TREES
CONIFERS

LANDSCAPE TREES

Trees, woody perennial plants growing to heights of 15–20 feet or more, are usually the largest and most dominant element in the landscape garden. Your site may already have an abundance of trees, and new landscapes and new plantings need to be planned carefully. The shape, size and growing habits of a tree will determine whether it is suitable for your site. Once established, trees are difficult to move, as their roots often spread out to two or three times the diameter of their outer branches.

Regardless of its form, learn how far your tree's branches will ultimately extend and to situate it accordingly. Keep in mind any overhanging wires or structures, competing plants and shadows to be cast by the mature specimen.

Landscape trees are classified according to type—evergreen or deciduous, broadleaved or conifer—or use—ornamental, shade or screen trees. Most landscape trees will look good whether planted alone, in groups, or in groves, but unusual specimens are better placed by themselves in sites appropriate to their scale and form. Position new trees carefully, using an overhead bubble diagram and an eye-level drawing of mature shapes (see pgs. 18–19).

If you have selected trees suited to your climate zone and site, major soil amendment should not be needed. The trees will adjust to the native soil. Nevertheless, improving drainage and grading before planting can improve a tree's chances. Pruning surface roots, limbs and branches will often improve a mature tree's appearance.

Japanese Yew

Taxus cuspidata

Slow dense growth, to 6 ft. high and 20 ft. wide in some varieties. Good for topiary. Sun or shade. Zones 4–8.

American Arborvitae

Thuja occidentalis

Narrow upright, grows to 60 ft. Full sun. Tolerates wet soil. Zones 2–7.

Dwarf White Spruce

Picea glauca 'comca'

Compact pyramidal tree. Slow growing to 7 ft. Short fine needles soft to the the touch. Zones 3–6.

Monterey Pine

Pinus radiata

Rapid growing with single or multiple trunks, to 60 ft. or more. Full sun in well-drained soil. Zones 7–10.

Pine

Pinus species

Widely varied group of single or multiple-trunk trees with grouped needles, 20–60 ft. or more tall. Full sun. Zones 2–9.

Colorado Blue Spruce

Picea pungens

Rigid, with graceful, open growth to 150 ft. or more. Dense needles circle branches. Full sun in moist, well-drained soil. Zones 4–8.

Douglas Fir

Pseudotsuga menziesii

Huge, with graceful, open growth to 150 ft. or more. Dense needles circle branches. Full sun in moist, well-drained soil. Zones 4–8.

Western Hemlock

Tsuga heterophylla

Rounded upright conical, grows to 100 ft. in cultivation. Needs moist soil. Zones 6–8 in West, 7–8 in East.

Italian Cypress

Cupressus sempervirens

Upright column, dark green, grows to 60 ft. Formal group or row plantings. Zones 7–9.

Monterey Cypress

Cupressus macrocarpa

Irregular or spreading upright, grows to 75 ft. or more. Salt tolerant, does best in seaside breezes. Zones 9-10.

Redwood

Sequoia sempervirens

Narrow upright conical form, fast-growing to 50 ft. in 15 years. Huge at maturity. Zones 7–10.

Southern Yew

Podocarpus macrophyllus

Rounded upright, good for screens, grows to 25 ft. Salt and shade tolerant. Zones 9–10.

TREES
DECIDUOUS TREES

TREES AND LAWNS

Lawns that contain trees or large shrubs require special attention. By shading the lawn and blocking the rain, trees and shrubs may rob the lawn of needed sunlight and nutrients. Tree leaves, if not raked from the lawn, often provide homes for pests and diseases. Most evergreens and some hardwoods may cause the soil to become too acidic. With a little care and planning, you can have wonderful shade trees and a beautiful lawn, too.

The biggest problem most trees cause for your lawn is shade. Most grasses do not grow as well without full sunlight. One way to solve the problem is to trim the tree, or tall shrub, to allow at least half of the sunlight to filter through. This can be done by carefully selecting the branches to be cut so the tree isn't disfigured. A second step you may want to take in shaded areas is to plant grass types that grow well without full sunlight. You can also reseed under trees using perennial ryegrass.

If you are planning your lawn and landscape, remember that deciduous trees that lose their leaves in winter provide excellent summer shade, but also require more work in autumn. Their leaves should be raked within a few days of falling because they provide pests and lawn diseases with perfect homes. They make good, acidic compost.

Almost all trees will form shallow surface roots if their only source of water is your lawn irrigation. Provide deep watering for your trees to prevent these surface roots from making your lawn unsightly.

Acacia

Acacia species

Good shade tree, irregular rounded shape, grows to 50 ft. Tolerates drought, poor soil and wind. Yellow flowers in spring. Zones 8–10.

Maple

Acer species

Tall, oval shade tree; grows to 100 ft. Brilliant scarlet to red-orange fall foliage. Moist, well-drained soil. Zones 3–8.

Japanese Maple

Acer palmatum

Small, decorative tree or shrub, to 8 ft. Full sun, part shade in warmer zones. Brilliant foliage, some throughout year. Zones 6–8.

Madrone

Arbutus menziesii

Spreading, rounded ornamental grows to 100 ft. Needs acid soil. Fruit in fall, winter. Zones 7–9.

Birch

Betua species

Graceful, gray-barked tree with small leaves that turn golden yellow in autumn. Part sun in moist soils, Zones 2–9.

Dogwood

Cornus species

Small flowering ornamental, grows to 30 ft. Blossoms in spring, fruit and scarlet foliage in fall. Zones 4–9.

Hawthorne

Crataegus species

Small, irregular form deciduous ornamental; grows to 25 ft. White flowers in spring, red berries in fall and winter. Zones 4–8.

Maidenhair Tree

Ginkgo biloba

Fan-shaped leaves turn brilliant yellow in fall, to 30 ft. Buy male trees to avoid messy, smelly fruit. Sun. Zones 4–9.

Redbud

Cercis species

Small deciduous ornamental, grows to 25 ft. Sun or part shade. Early spring red or white flowers. Zones 5–9.

Gum Eucalyptus

Eucalyptus species

Narrow, upright aromatic evergreen; grows to 100 ft. Drought tolerant, well-drained soil only. Zones 9–10.

Thornless Honey Locust

Gleditsia tricanthos

Slow growth of plume-like foliage, to 60 ft. Yellow fall color. Full sun in moist soil. Zones 4–9.

TREES
DECIDUOUS TREES

American Holly

Ilex species

Broadleaf evergreen, conical when young, grows to 50 ft. Accepts salt, needs shade and moist soil. Red berries in fall and winter. Zones 4–7.

American Sweet Gum

Liquidambar styraciflua

Deciduous ornamental and shade tree, grows to 75 ft. Brilliant yellow and scarlet leaves in fall. Tolerates wet soil. Zones 5–9.

Flowering Crab Apple

Malus floribunda

Small rounded ornamental, grows to 25 ft. Pink-white spring blossoms, fall fruit. Zones 4–7.

Canary Islands Date Palm

Phoenix canariensis

Ornamental palm, grows to 60 ft. Hardy, fruit in fall, winter. Full sun. Zones 9–10.

Sweet Bay, Laurel

Laurus nobilis

Triangular broadleaf ornamental, grows to 20–40 ft. Well-drained soil; tolerates drought when mature. Zones 7–9.

Southern Magnolia

Magnolia grandiflora

Large evergreen, classic ornamental and shade tree, grows to 80 ft. Moist soil, shade. Zones 7–9.

Olive

Olea europea

Drought-tolerant ornamental, grows to 30 ft. Fruit in winter, spring; 'Fruitless' cultivar is less messy. Zones 9–10, semihardy Zone 8.

Weeping Willow

Salix alba

Popular spreading willow, grows to 70 ft. Tolerates wetness. Zones 2–8.

Callery Pear

Pyrus calleryana 'Bradford'

Medium-sized triangular ornamental; grows to 50 ft. White flowers in spring, fruit in summer, scarlet-purple foliage in fall. Zones 4–8.

Oak

Quercus species

Large, slow-growing shade tree, to 90 ft. or more tall. Full sun in acidic, well-drained soil. Zones 3–9.

Pagoda Tree

Sophora japonica

Rounded ornamental, grows to 70 ft. Yellow-white flowers in summer; fruit in fall, winter. Zones 4–8.

Littleleaf Linden

Tilia cordata

Handsome, gray bark on quick-growing, upright tree, to 70 ft. Small yellow flowers with rich scent. Full sun. Zones 3–8.

Oriental Cherry

Prunus serrulata

Vase-shaped upright ornamental, grows to 30 ft. Pink flowers in spring, orange foliage color in fall. Full sun, moist soil. Zones 5–9.

California Live Oak

Quercus agrifolia

Rounded evergreen, fast-growing, irregular spreading shapes. Grows to 80 ft. Full sun. Zones 8–10.

European Mountain Ash

Sorbus aucuparia

Deciduous ornamental, grows to 30 ft. Spring blossoms, fall berries. Needs well-drained acid soil. Zones 3–7.

Cactus and Other Succulent Plants

Arid Landscapes

Cactus and other succulent plants are natural landscape elements in the hot, arid regions of the southwestern United States, but some hardier types can thrive in more temperate regions if sheltered. The dramatic forms and textures of taller cactus and succulents make striking silhouettes against the earth and sky in open landscapes, while low-growing succulents can serve as ornaments for rocks, walls and crevices.

While desert plants have a well-deserved reputation for being drought-resistant, many are quite sensitive to water, temperature and soil nutrient conditions. They generally need full sun, well-drained soil and balanced soil to grow and flower profusely. Cactus and succulents dry out in very hot climates if their root systems are not well established. Don't assume that these tough-looking plants are immune to insect and soil pests, either— they suffer from insect pests and diseases just like temperate-climate plants.

Ice plant succulents are well suited for groundcovers. Many grow in a wide range of climates. Flowering specimens are adaptable to a wide range of landscape surfaces and require very little soil preparation. Others are ideally suited for loose or sandy soil conditions or for covering steep slopes unsuited for lawns or flower beds. Ice plants are also useful for controlling erosion.

CAUTION

Never remove native plants from the wild.

Century Plant

Agave americana

Long, stiff leaves to 6 ft., flower stalk to 40 ft. high with 2 1/2 in. flowers on top. Blooms and dies. Zone 10.

Aloe

Aloe nobilis

Dark green leaves edged with small hooked teeth. Clustered orange-red flowers on 2 ft. stalks in June. Zones 9–10.

Agave

Agave attenuata

Ornamental garden or park plant, spreading swordlike leaves up to 5 ft. long. Green and yellow 2 in. flowers. Needs moist sandy loam, good drainage. Zones 9–10.

Saguaro

Carnegiea gigantea

Very large columnar form, branches in wild, less frequently in garden. Slow-growing to 60 ft., native of Southwest. Zone 10.

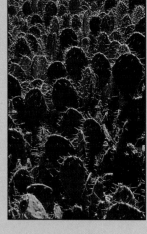

Old Man Cactus

Cephalocerius senilis

Long, white, silky hairs conceal spines. The Old Man can grow to 50 ft. Zone 10.

Hens and Chicks

Echeveria species

Hardy, blue-green rosettes 4–6 in. across, with yellow-white flowers in fall or winter. Zones 4–10.

Cow's Horn

Euphorbia grandicornis

Twisting, wavy branches with brown-gray spines, grows to 6 ft., often in pairs. Sun, winter temps. above 50 degrees. Zone 10.

Prickly Pear

Opuntia species

Upright, growing to 4 ft. Flat, oval blue-green pads, pink-red flowers. Any well-drained soil. Zone 4–10.

Silver Torch

Cleisocactus Strausii

Columnar, dense silver-white spines, trunk to 2 1/2 in. wide, 6 ft. high. Deep red flowers. Zones 9–10.

Golden Barrel Cactus

Echinocactus grusonii

Popular spherical cactus, reaches 3 ft. or more in diameter. Golden-yellow spines, small red flowers. Zone 10.

Ice Plant

Lampranthus

Succulent subshrub with blindingly brilliant large flowers. Plant in full sun. Needs little or no summer water. Zones 6–9.

Yucca

Yucca recurvifolia

Stiff, swordlike blue-gray leaves with yellow center stripe, grows 8 ft. high from clump. Zones 8–10.

FERNS

Ferns are woodland natives with green, feathery fronds. Most have the same basic needs—rich, acidic (pH 5 to 6) soil of leaf mold and regular watering. Late spring mulching will keep roots cool and suppress weeds; spring and fall composting will restore nutrients lost to competing nearby plants.

Maidenhair Fern

Adiantum pedatum

Reaches 24 in. in height. Full shade. Zones 3–8.

Lady Fern

Athyrium filix-femma

Reaches 3 ft. Wide, sharply cut fronds make good detail plant. Likes full sun, woods soil, some lime. Zones 3–8.

Japanese Holly Fern

Cyrotomium falcatum

Stiff fronds reach 2 1/2 ft. in length. Zones 9–10.

Ostrich Fern

Matteuccia pennsylvanica

Reaches 5 ft. or more in length. Likes rich, loamy soil. Zones 3–7.

Hedge Fern

Polystichum setiferum

Low-growing fern with spreading finely-cut fronds make for a lacy plant. Regular summer water. Hardy to zone 7.

Tasmanian Tree Fern

Dicksonia antarctica

Part or full shade. Handsome large woody trunk to 5 ft. Zones 9–10.

Royal Fern

Osmunda regalis

Grows up to 6 ft. Likes shade, needs moist acid soil to thrive. Zones 3–8.

Chain Fern

Woodwardica species

Found wild from Nova Scotia to Florida, grow to 2 ft. Full sun. Zones 5–9.

Woodfern

Dryopteris species

Found in wild from northeast U.S. to Arkansas. Grows 2–2 1/2 ft. high. Full or part shade. Zones 3–9.

Polypody Wall Fern

Polypodium vulgare

Grows to 10 in. high, fronds to 18 in. Full or part shade. Zones 3–9.

LANDSCAPES OVER TIME

PLANNING LANDSCAPES THAT LAST

After you've designed your landscape and selected your plants, the job of planning is still not complete. Visualize how your landscape will look years down the road simply by imagining what would happen if you let nature take over. Native plants begin to reappear wherever they are not kept out; perennials spread and bunch out; young shrubs and trees grow steadily until they reach maturity. As screen and shade trees grow to full size, shade-loving plants will emerge below them and sun-loving plants will disappear.

All of your plants, native and cultivated, are subject to the natural cycle of growth, change and renewal in the landscape. In the best-planned gardens, the original choice of landscape plants works within a steadily developing environment of vegetation and new specimens. With time, hedges take shape, groundcovers spread and form a mat, and screen shrubs and trees close and intertwine their branches. Slow-growing shrubs and trees may take many years to reach the size you visualized in your landscape plan, so buy the largest specimens you can afford and place them far enough apart to not crowd each other.

Many landscape plants and most lawns eventually reach the end of their lifecycle and require renewal or replacement. If you plan your landscape wisely and maintain it well, however, you will get many years of use and enjoyment from your original plantings.

Bareroot Maple (*Acer* species)

Boxwood (*Buxus* species)

Lilyturf (*Liriope* species)

After One Year

After Five Years

67

PREPARING TO PLANT

Plant border and edging

Turfgrass

Water service

Topsoil

Subsoil

Roots

68

CONDUCTING A SOIL TEST

Soil tests measure the amount of nutrients your garden soil has available for your plants, and tell you which fertilizers you need to add for good growth and heavy flowering. You can test soil for many things, but the four basic soil tests are for chemical content—nitrogen, phosphorus, potassium—and pH (acidity or alkalinity).

Nitrogen (N) is needed to produce leaf growth and good chlorophyll. Phosphorus (P) promotes growth of root systems, and stimulates flower and seed formation. Potassium or potash (K) carries carbohydrates throughout the entire plant, building strength and resistance to disease. The pH test measures the overall acidity or alkalinity of the soil.

Mark the location of each soil sample if you are testing a large landscape area. For smaller gardens, mix several samples together to obtain an average sample. Send the sample or samples to a nearby agricultural extension or soil lab. You'll need to be able to properly interpret the results. N, P and K test results are usually expressed as the percentages of nitrogen, phosphorus and potassium fertilizer needed. Fortunately, these percentages are also the three numbers found on the labeling of most fertilizers.

Your pH test result will translate into the amount of lime or sulfur needed to bring the soil back into the desired range. You can actually fine-tune the soil's pH to your plants' individual requirements. For example, most turfgrasses prefer neutral to slightly acid soil (pH 6.5–7.0), ferns like more acidic soil (pH 5.0–6.0). Familiarize yourself with the basics of soil structure and composition before applying fertilizers, lime or sulfur, so you'll know how much soil to turn over for the best results.

PLANTING SMALL LANDSCAPE PLANTS

Smaller plants, groundcovers and container-grown shrubs can all serve as a quick means to fill in bare areas in the landscape. A little extra care before planting will help them grow and spread rapidly. Take care to water and fertilize plants as needed while they are getting established.

Groundcovers

First Clear soil surface, turn soil to 1 ft. if possible. Spread layer of organic compost over surface, turn into soil.

Then Rake level, water to settle soil. Set plants out in staggered rows. Dig holes with trowel or shovel. Loosen roots, place in holes.

Last Refill the holes halfway, water to settle, finish filling. Water regularly, soaking roots and avoiding foliage, until established.

Transplants

First Dig holes twice as wide and deep as plants, loosen soil and mix with organic compost and all-purpose fertilizer.

Then Remove plants from container, pushing from bottom. Cut any encircling roots, loosen rootball. Place plant in hole, position to ground level.

Last Fill with improved soil, firm soil around plant. Water well, reposition plants if necessary.

5-Gallon Containers

First Dig hole twice as wide and deep as container, set aside topsoil on tarp. Mix topsoil with organic compost.

Then Place soil in bottom of hole to height where plant will be level or just above ground level. Remove shrub carefully from container, holding by rootball.

Last Place shrub in hole, position. Fill halfway with soil, water well to soak rootball. Fill and firm soil.

PLANTING LARGE LANDSCAPE PLANTS

Large plants and trees act as backdrops, screens or walls in your garden. These woody plants may be purchased either bare-root or container-grown. Young bare-root trees appear in stores near planting time—it differs for each climate area. Older, container-grown trees are available all year. Choose bare-root or container-grown plants by your plan and budget.

Bare-Root Plantings

First Prune away any damage or disease. Dig hole 6 in. beyond roots' width and height at old soil line.

Then Mix 0–10–0 fertilizer with soil from hole. Mound soil under roots until the soil line is 1 in. above ground.

Last Press roots to firm soil. Backfill halfway. Settle with water, allow to seep in. Finish fill, mound soil basin.

Container Plantings

First Lay tree on side, loosen rootball with trowel. Moisten. Slide container from ball. Avoid pulling trunk.

Then Cut any circling roots with knife. Dig hole 6 in. wider than rootball at depth equal to old soil line.

Last Add 4 oz. 0–10–0 fertilizer to native soil. Hold rootball, position soil line at ground surface. Fill and water.

Boxed Specimen Trees

First Transport to site. Dig hole 1 ft. larger than box. Dismantle box with pry bar and remove. Cut circling roots.

Then Hold tree by rootball, not trunk. Slide into hole without lifting or breaking rootball. **Caution**: *very heavy!*

Last Level to soil surface. Backfill around rootball, mound basin around tree. Fertilize with 0–10–0, water.

Basic Pruning and Landscape Care

Caring for the landscape is a year-round task. Some plants require special maintenance at particular times, while others need only periodic care. Trees and shrubs often require very little help beyond occasional pruning; many evergreen trees rarely need upkeep. Most other trees need regular winter inspection and pruning. Cut fruit trees back about one-quarter while dormant in January or February. Deciduous shade trees may need pruning of limbs and surface roots in late autumn or winter. Late autumn and early winter are the best times to clean up soil surfaces and remove debris.

In spring, prune your deciduous and evergreen flowering shrubs. Cut back stems and pinch off shoots to encourage spring and summer blossoms. Pinch evergreen flowering shrubs back to shape in late spring—never prune them after mid-summer. Prune deciduous flowering shrubs to shape after blooms fade—trim back old stems and branches from the center of the plant in late summer.

Major pruning of evergreen hedges and screens should wait until plants are dormant. Early fall is the time to prune sugar maple, magnolia and walnut trees; most other deciduous trees can be pruned safely throughout the dormant season.

Spray any trees or shrubs that need winter dormant oil and anti-dessicants to prevent drying. Winterize roses and other delicate plants with straw, burlap or other coverings in cold climates.

Pruning Deciduous Trees and Shrubs

First Use lopping shears to remove any dead, weakened or diseased branches. Cut back to junction of branch.

Next Thin any crossing branches and stems with shears or saw. Light will reach inner branches and leaves to promote growth.

Last Cut back 1/4–1/3 of new growth for shape, using pruning shears; make cuts above outside buds so new stems grow away from trunk.

Hybrid Tea Rose Annual Pruning

First Prune away dead or damaged canes, cutting close to the base at a 45° angle. Cut weak or dead stems back to junction with canes.

Next Cut healthy canes back at 45° angle, 1/4–1/2 in. above outside bud. Prune for shape, nipping off tips.

Last Remove any suckers from the rootstock. Water.

Shaping Fine-Leaved Hedges

First Cut away dead branches in front of smaller branches. To thin, reach inside outer foliage with pruning shears and cut side branches.

Next For formal hedges, set a string between stakes as a guide to the desired height. Let plant grow to string.

Last Using hedge shears, trim the foliage wider at the bottom than at the top, or round off at the top.

LANDSCAPING TOOLS

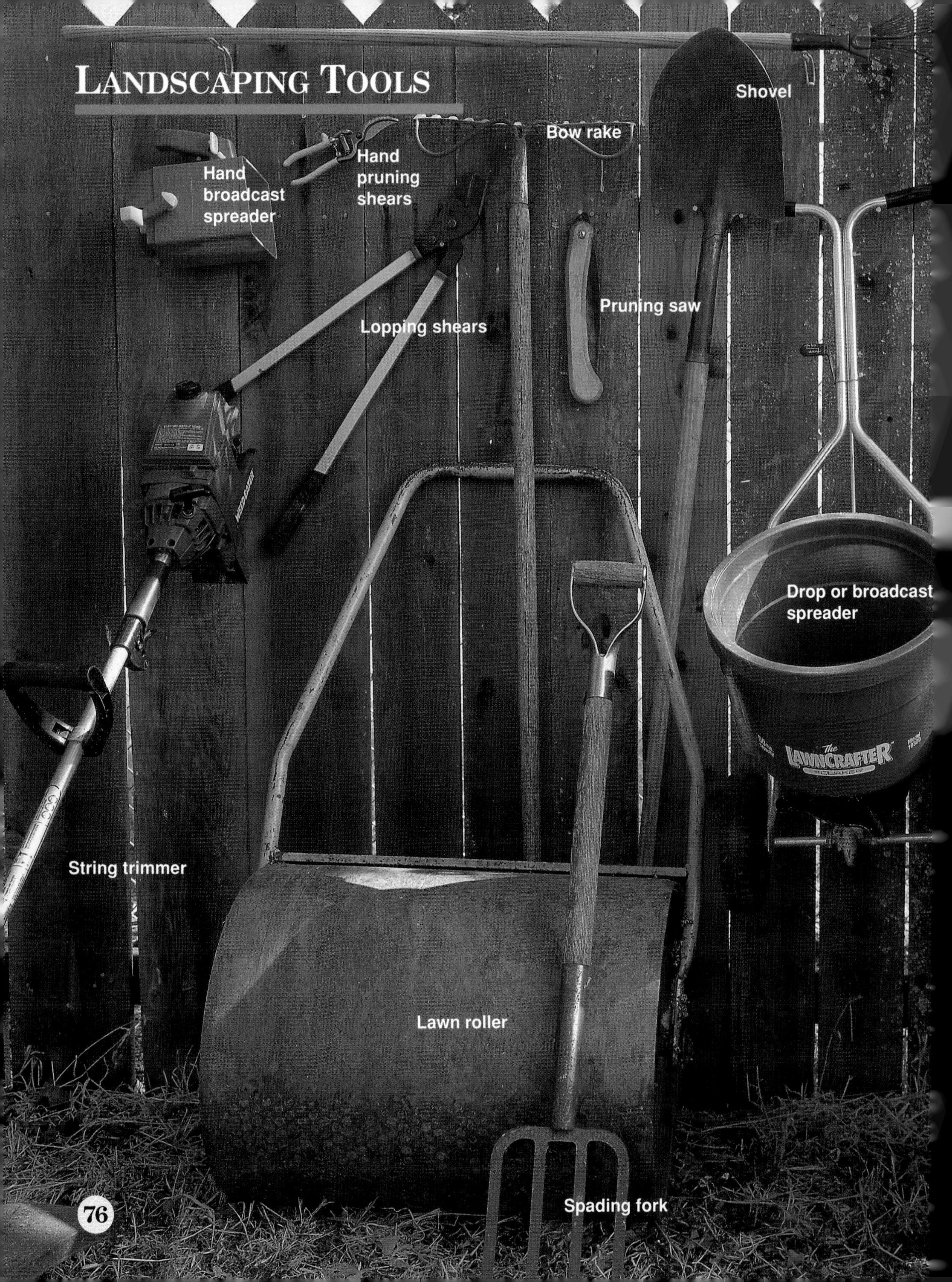

Hand broadcast spreader

Hand pruning shears

Lopping shears

Bow rake

Shovel

Pruning saw

Drop or broadcast spreader

The LAWNCRAFTER

String trimmer

Lawn roller

Spading fork

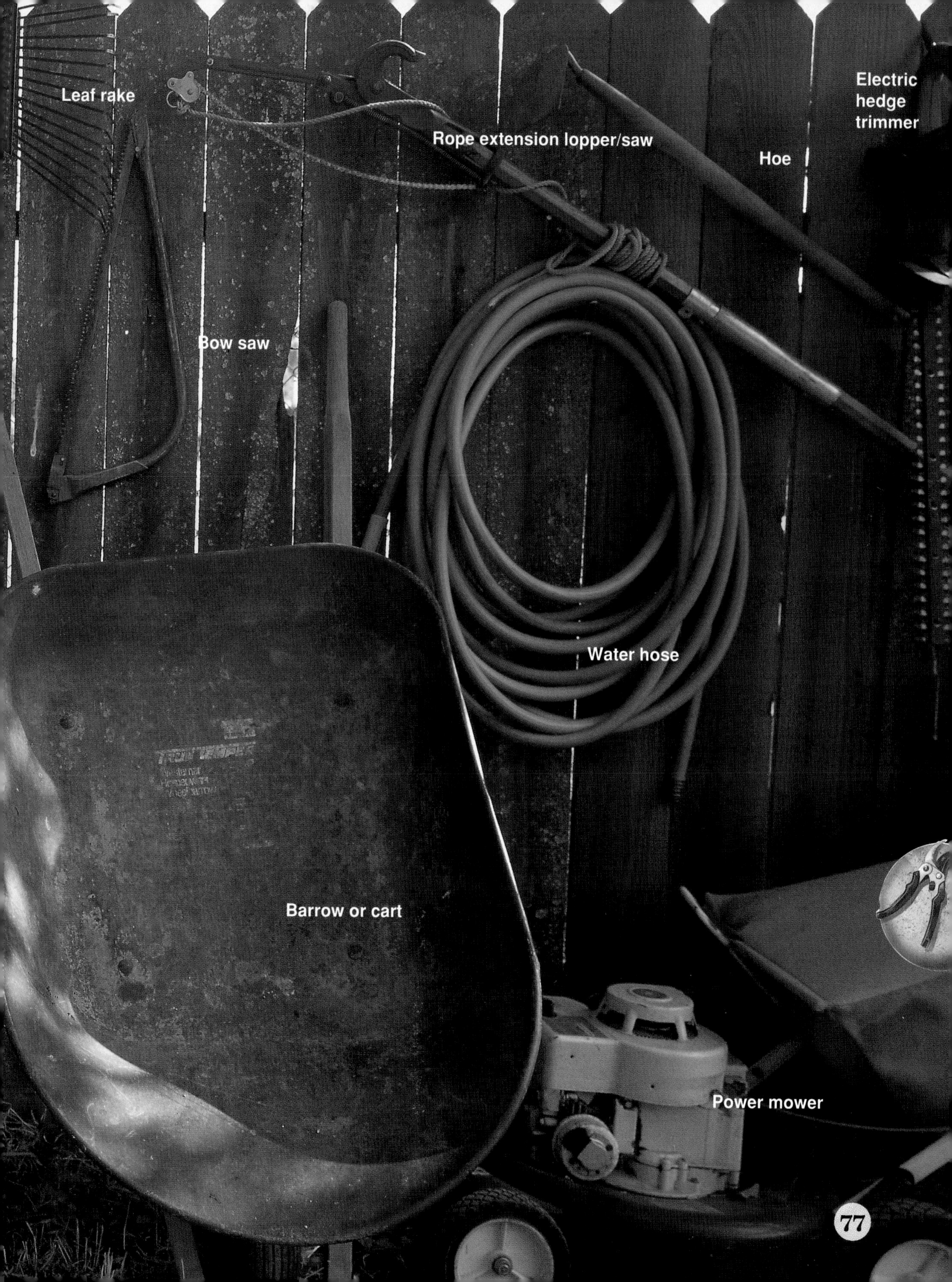

Leaf rake

Rope extension lopper/saw

Hoe

Electric
hedge
trimmer

Bow saw

Water hose

Barrow or cart

Power mower

BIBLIOGRAPHY AND INDEX